CONTEMPORARY COTTAGES

CONTEMPORARY COTTAGES

MOLLY HYDE ENGLISH

Photographs by RYAN GARVIN

GIBBS SMITH
TO ENRICH AND INSPIRE HUMANKIND

To my husband, Rich, and to all of our pups: those departed—Maggie, Hannah, Charlie, Buddy, Tipper, and Lily—as well as our two "fur-kids," Emma and Molly, who have sat patiently at my feet as I have planned and prepared this book. My sincere love and gratitude. —Molly Hyde English

To my uncle Jeff, who would have been so proud to display this book on his coffee table. —Ryan Garvin

Text © 2019 Molly Hyde English
Photographs © 2019 Ryan Garvin

Published by
Gibbs Smith
P.O. Box 667
Layton, Utah 84041

1.800.835.4993 orders
www.gibbs-smith.com

Designed by Sheryl Dickert
Printed and bound in China

Gibbs Smith books are printed on either recycled, 100% post-consumer waste, FSC-certified papers or on paper produced from sustainable PEFC-certified forest/controlled wood source. Learn more at www.pefc.org.

Library of Congress Cataloging-in-Publication Data

Names: English, Molly Hyde, author. | Garvin, Ryan, photographer.
Title: Contemporary cottages / Molly Hyde English ; photographs by Ryan Garvin.
Description: First edition. | Layton, Utah : Gibbs Smith, [2019]
Identifiers: LCCN 2018039594 | ISBN 9781423651376 (jacketless hardcover)
Subjects: LCSH: Cottages--United States. | Second homes--United States. |
    Vacation homes--United States. | Interior decoration--United States.
Classification: LCC NA7561 .E537 2019 | DDC 728/.370973--dc23
LC record available at https://lccn.loc.gov/2018039594

First Edition
23 22 21 20 19   5 4 3 2 1

CONTENTS

ACKNOWLEDGMENTS

As I contemplated a final book—the last in a trilogy of Gibbs Smith books dedicated to the American cottage—it was a call to action by a fellow merchant, Laurie Alter, founder and owner of the ever-popular Tuvalu Design, that led to *Contemporary Cottages*. Laurie had stopped by my store, Camps and Cottages, to say hello and peek at a gallery-framed U.S. forty-eight-star vintage flag that I had just installed. Laurie and husband, Jeff, had recently completed work on a contemporary cottage and she noted that there was a perfect place in the cottage for the flag. Intrigued, I asked her if I might visit what was at one time a half-century-old ranch which had been given new life as a contemporary cottage and new home for Laurie, Jeff and son, Cody. I dropped by a few days later and she was right. The flag was a perfect fit but more importantly their work on the cottage convinced me that a third book had to be done! If the inspirational visit were not enough, Laurie suggested I contact photographer Ryan Garvin who jumped at the opportunity and who has worked so professionally and diligently on the project. Thank you, Ryan!

Many of the owners have asked to remain anonymous. To all of you, it's my hope that the photos have pleased each of you and more importantly I wish to thank you for sharing your thoughts, insights and ideas with readers. You may very well inspire others to give new life to their cottages in the future.

Stories about several of the cottages were shared with me by their designers. To Raili Clasen, Kelly Nutt, Shannon Wilkins, Mindy Laven and Ashley Clark—my sincere appreciation and best wishes to each of you for continued success with your design businesses.

A special acknowledgement and thank you to Michele Graham, founder and owner of Juxtaposition Home, one of the West Coast's great stores, who suggested candidate cottages and worked with me on a number of project photo shoots.

Finally and most importantly I wish to give a very appreciative acknowledgment to Madge Baird, managing editor at Gibbs Smith, for her patience and perseverance in putting me to the test to ensure that we crossed the finish line.

INTRODUCTION

Change is not merely necessary to life—it is life.

—ALVIN TOFFLER, *FUTURE SHOCK**

With the publication of both *Camps and Cottages* in 2000 and *Vintage Cottages* in 2007, I became increasingly aware that the concept of "cottage," one of many types of structures Americans call home, was at the cusp of a back-to-the-future stage of its life as a distinct architectural style—a style born for the most part in the early twentieth century. Unlike the grand homes of that period, followed by the craftsman-inspired bungalows of the 1920s, the ranch homes of post-WW II suburbia, the glass and steel curations of the early 1960s, stuccos of the 1970s and 1980s and the ever-popular McMansions of the early 2000s (a style that has receded due partly to the Great Recession of 2007 and partly to a return to realistic scale), the cottage has maintained its form, fit and function with a focus on charm, beauty, uniqueness, human scale and relative affordability. In fact, community leaders in my hometown, a town known nationally for its environmental focus, historic preservation and respect for the arts, have chosen for many years to focus upon its cottages with two annual events— "The Charm Tour" and "The Garden Tour."**

That having been said, as we approach the end of the second decade of the new century, cottage owners (and those who yearn to be) have begun to

lend imaginative touches to the traditional image of an American cottage. Though, understandably for professional designers, there may be some very distinct differences between what is defined as "contemporary" and what is understood as "modern," it's apparent from the projects undertaken by the owners of the cottages featured on the following pages that one school of design is as equally attractive to them as the other, while others have worked to marry a contemporary and modern look with touches of traditional and vintage—a true juxtaposition of styles linking the past, present and future. The owners featured in *Contemporary Cottages* have burnished traditional features with fresh and modern appointments, responsible landscaping, magical entryways, updated and repurposed rooms, open ceilings, custom floor plans and unique lighting—all without disturbing the timeless charm and scale that defines a cottage.

Contemporary Cottages is more than just a tour of handsome cottages; it welcomes you, the reader, into each home as if you were on a walking tour with a personal guide, including insightful conversations with each owner as they share the dreams, thoughts and imagination that went into the design or redesign of their cottage. Note the personal description of each cottage and how it reflects the owners' personalities and lifestyle, the inspiration for the cottage's design, the unique characteristics or features, the owners' experience with the builder, interior designer or architect—what they learned from their experience working with outside professionals— and what led to the owners' choice of color schemes seen throughout each cottage. A particularly interesting feature within the cottages is the presence of art—whether in the form of paintings, artistic photos, object d'art or sculpture—inside and outside the property. Owners of cottages in cultures and countries much older than ours have for years traditionally and tastefully appointed their cottages in an artful way and it appears that this practice is growing in the U.S. with an increasing willingness by homeowners to pursue tasteful and original art in place of reproductions and manufactured appointments. It is a practice similar to the world of fine dining where it is not unusual for a respected chef to suggest the accompaniment of her award-winning 2019 cuisine with wine(s) that have been carefully maintained in temperature-controlled cellars for years or decades, waiting for the perfect pairing—the perfect moment.

A wise person once noted that the hallmark of a measured and balanced life is one's ability to draw together the dreams of the past with the thoughts of the day and images of the future. It appears that each owner has achieved that balance and it is my pleasure to welcome you into their world—through the magic of *Contemporary Cottages*.

Molly English
2019
Laguna Beach, California

* Toffler, Alvin, *Future Shock,* New York: Random House., 1970

** Laguna Beach, CA. www.villagelaguna.org/charm-house-tour/ and www.lagunabeachgardenclub.org/gate-garden-tour/

COASTAL RANCH

Create your own visual style . . . let it be unique for yourself and yet identifiable for others.

—ORSON WELLES

D isregard for conformity" were words chosen by Mark Christy, brother of cottage owner Laurie Alter, in describing Hobie Alter, Laurie's father-in-law, at a 2014 memorial honoring the surfing and sailing industry legend shortly after his passing. "I, like every member of the Alter family, have been touched and influenced by Hobie's legacy—one built upon the principles of taking a different road, charting a new route and paving a course for new ideas."

So it is with the approach Laurie took in the redesign of a cottage for her own family in what began as a circa 1960s coast-side cottage. "As owner as well as designer, my focus is built on a thoughtful and eclectic sensibility—neither on impulse nor on trends. As a designer, I begin each project with a study of its owners (in this case a lot of introspection and collaboration with my husband), their style, vibe and what they wish to accomplish." As a leading merchant and designer, Laurie has made it a habit of planning well in advance her next move—both in business and in design. The transformation of the half-century-old house into a cottage befitting the new millennium was no exception. Her project started with "over-pulls" of tile from which to select just the right color, pattern and design for the cottage. "Eighteen months transpired between the first day we applied pencil to paper until the day we moved in. It was quite a challenge to turn the darkish, fifty-year-old structure into a more open and comfortable place. As if that were not enough, we immediately determined that it was out of square, adding to extra challenges in the placement of hardwood floors, use of shiplap walls and the construction of a tongue and groove ceiling—but we got it done!"

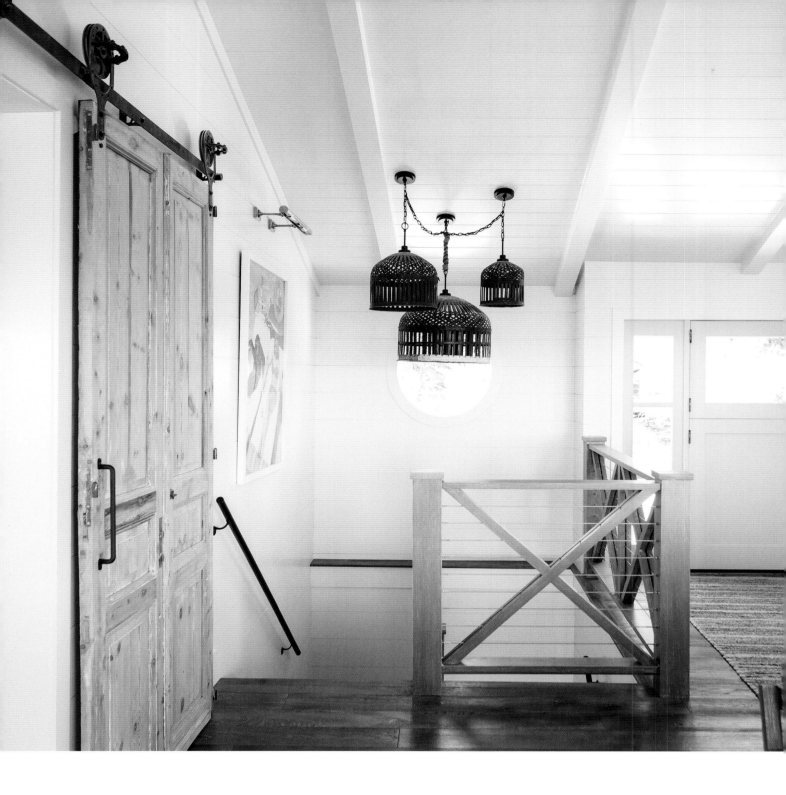

Laurie commissioned original lighting for several areas of the home,
including this trio of hanging shades made from vintage bird cages.

Laurie thought through every structural detail of the cottage while attending to the eventual design of its interior as a place of consistency, warmth and quality. The darkness was replaced with a Benjamin Moore designer white shade but with her insistence that an abundance of color and accents be added in the form of area rugs, art and fabrics. "We are a family whose life has been shaped by the ocean—by a cadence of ebb and flow that is both unique and perpetual. The goal was to create a clean and uncomplicated living space consistent with the lessons we have learned each day from our interaction with and respect for the sea."

ABOVE: "Surf's Up!" is the theme in the family's expansive kitchen and open-air dining area.

OPPOSITE: Clean lines associated with all of Laurie's cabinetry reflect her focus on utility and beauty.

The cottage's blend of uniqueness and simplicity is apparent the moment one walks unto the property and enters the cottage. "As with many of my projects before and after my own cottage, I worked with Low Country Originals. They designed an oyster and beach glass chandelier in the dining area. We discovered a number of compelling pieces at the Texas Round Top Antique Show and put them to good use by way of custom lighting made from upside-down antique pigeon cages. We bought old cowboy flannel shirts and shadow-boxed them for placement in the kids' rooms." Even more interesting is the unconventional and unique path that Laurie and her husband took in building their cottage. They first conceptualized how they wished to live and what they wished to live with, followed by a search for intriguing and curated architectural elements, including a set of vintage Hungarian entry doors, rubbed-bronze pieces and steel hardware.

ABOVE: The repurposed bass drum from a '60s rock band makes the perfect table for this room.

OPPOSITE: Vintage beams, wide-planked hardwood and an antique basket complement the contemporary look.

The use of stone and timber juxtaposed against the clean lines of board and batten provides the Alter family's guests with an architectural treat—traditional elements highlighted against a backdrop of twenty-first-century *toucher*. On each floor one finds a splash of color, shape and form. From the beamed ceiling living room upon entry, complete with a floor-to-ceiling stone fireplace, the journey continues through a large timbered door, which opens in an east-west fashion using industrial-size pulleys and rails, to an equally impressive kitchen, dining area and great room sporting wall-to-wall windows that capture sunlight from dawn to dusk. A hardwood staircase with a geometrically designed guard railing leads to the living quarters of a series of airy and unique bed and bath rooms.

OPPOSITE: A massive driftwood-framed mirror, antique bench peeking from a cover and a bedside lamp encircled with puka shells lend a coastal vibe to the master bedroom.

BELOW AND RIGHT: The en suite bathroom looks beautiful from any angle.

Laurie has used her standing as a respected merchant to appoint the cottage with furniture, textiles, fixtures and objects that have combined, though often in contradictory ways, to complete her vision. "We made great effort to steer clear of catalogues, preferring instead to deal with local businesses, custom crafts people and one-of-a-kind vendors—seeking to make each vignette within the cottage a space that grabs you and reminds you that this is home."

Following the inspiration of her iconic father-in-law, Laurie and Jeff have built their coastal ranch by taking a different road and in doing so have paved a course to a comfortable and unique contemporary cottage experience.

OPPOSITE: Laurie has chosen early-twentieth-century fixtures for this guest bathroom.
ABOVE: Flannel cowboy shirts in shadow boxes make statement wall art for a kids' room.

PENINSULA POINT

There are always new, grander challenges to confront, and a true winner will embrace each one.

—MIA HAMM

Like the successful designers with whom she has worked and admired, Raili Clasen has been up to the challenge in each project she has taken on. California born and raised, Raili has firmly embedded her focus and sensibility in a period of time when the Golden State displayed to the rest of the world a civic fabric of unbridled possibilities with a sun that never set.

After college and a few starter jobs, she landed a key marketing position with a global surf apparel manufacturer. "Being in the industry was like earning a second degree and I learned very quickly that, though steeped in a beach vibe, it was, at the end of the day, all business. I also learned very quickly the importance of proposal development, deadlines and client satisfaction and that if I wanted to make design my career in the form of interior design, I needed to marry my creative eye with critical business skills."

This quintessential cottage is a getaway for a couple who spends much of their time exploring the history and cultural wonders of the world while always looking forward to returning to home base—and to their four grown children and four grandchildren. The seaside cottage, akin to a Cape Cod and one of several owned over the years by the family, was built in the 1930s. The owners made it clear at their first meeting with Clasen that they had a strong point of view related to design. "We knew exactly what we had and more importantly precisely what we wanted to do—and not do. We didn't want to change the cottage's nature nor its face to a point that it faced losing its original character. Instead, we asked Raili to help us give the wonderful place new life while working with its existing bones."

The owners took a minimalist approach with furniture. Multiple visits to Scandinavia had made them comfortable with a functional and natural approach to furniture, along with textiles that exhibit movement and intriguing lines.

"That approach was exactly what I had hoped to hear," says Clasen, looking back on that initial meeting. "Though more than three-quarters of a century old, it had a simple yet solid presence and was obviously made to withstand sand and sea as well as the wear and tear of large family gatherings each summer season." There were immediate challenges—some large and some facial. An immediate target for face-lift was the bathroom lighting. Says Clasen, "My client and I felt the best way to overcome that challenge was to introduce ceiling lighting with dimmer control." To do so required reconfiguration of the ceiling, which was accomplished with a three-inch drop and introduction of sunken lighting within the drop area. Upon completion of the installation and an earlier walk-through, the owner, with some of his grandchildren in hand, immediately headed to the bathroom, looked at Raili and gleefully exclaimed, "Mission accomplished!"

Similar to cottages of the period, the ceilings throughout the main living areas were low by today's standards, leaving the rooms light challenged. The owner voiced concern saying, "We live in an area that is blessed with more than 300 days of sunshine each year. We asked Raili to do what she could to make better use of the natural light." Clasen responded by raising the ceiling of the single-story cottage into the attic space and the result was immediate—the main living area was flooded in natural sunlight, which continued throughout the rest of the cottage. To enhance the lightness the owners chose a Benjamin Moore designer white throughout. Cautious of how overwhelming a white interior can be, Clasen elected to contrast the trim and a number of bedroom walls with Benjamin Moore's "Wrought Iron"—a shade of black—dark, but not starkly so.

OPPOSITE: The juxtaposed Kerry Rosenthal-designed wallpaper and complementary bedding reflect the owners' taste for the diverse cultures explored on their global travels.

ABOVE: Bathrooms infuse character with a Rorschach-like pattern of stars and diamonds.

The grandchildren's rooms are alive with colors. In one bedroom, large blue polka dots fill two walls—totally unexpected yet complementary to the clean lines throughout the rest of the cottage.

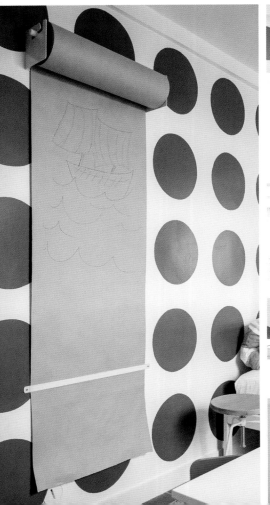

Seeking to complement the brightness of the interior, the owners elected to declutter and take a minimal-ist approach with furniture. "We had visited Scandinavia often and had grown comfortable with their func-tional and natural approach to furniture along with textiles that exhibit movement and intriguing lines. The grandchildren's rooms are alive with yellows, industrial wall letters, typography and murals and in one bed-room large blue polka dots fill two walls—a design totally unexpected and yet complementary to the clean and efficient lines found throughout the rest of the cottage."

"Having lightened the inside of our cottage, we pondered how best to treat the outside. The cottage sports original sixteen-inch redwood shingles that are extremely costly to replace but if properly maintained will last a lifetime. The shingles were original to the cottage and we wished to preserve them." After consulting with Clasen, the owners elected to repair shingles that were cracked and then hand-painted all of them with several coats of the Benjamin Moore "Wrought Iron" that not only protected them against the sand and sea air but set the cottage apart from nearby homes in a unique and respectful manner. Designer Clasen notes, "To top off the boldness of the Wrought Iron, we introduced a dark black Dutch door with copper outdoor lighting and accented the lines of the roof with copper rain gutters that will patina beautifully over time, ensuring that the cottage maintains its timeless appeal."

As toasts were made on move-in day the owner exclaimed, "To own a cottage with nearly a century under its belt is to own a treasure. We, the current generation of owners, are expected to maintain its sense of originality and tradition and we thank Raili Clasen for transforming our ideas into reality to do just that!"

SHORES REDUX

You've always had the power, my dear, you just had to learn it by yourself.

—GLINDA'S WORDS TO DOROTHY IN *THE WIZARD OF OZ,* 1939

When the phone rang in designer Mindy Laven's office, it was from the party she had hoped would call. It had been several days from their first contact, and it was Mindy's hope that she had provided the family with the assurance that she was the person who could turn what they called their half-century-old "hodge-podge" home into a twenty-first-century contemporary cottage. From the voice of the owner came the words she was hoping to hear, "Mindy—we were excited when it became apparent to us at our recent meeting that of all the designers we have interviewed you understood best our desire to retain the classic look of the original cottage and to build on that look. You seemed to understand best the fact that we wished to retain something that reflects the essence of the original house—its soul—and to honor its structure. You understood us. The project is yours!" After the call, Laven couldn't help but reflect on her life in central Ohio. "I wanted to be an artist or art teacher but my Dad, with no disrespect for careers in art or education, told me that I was just too smart to teach and I had the power to achieve," she notes. "But in a way I really have learned much by myself and have become a teacher of sorts—by helping clients understand that the most compelling design is one that incorporates the best elements of the past with the comfort and functionality of the present."

Laven has done that with Shores Redux, in collaboration with the current owners. The half-century-old structure has provided her with a perfect palate upon which to build a twenty-first-century cottage. The owners, who are multilingual and have traveled the globe, noted, "The house is in an established and venerated neighborhood and prior to our purchase was owned by one family for all of those years. We were looking to infuse it with new life while maintaining the solid bones upon which it was built."

"We told Mindy that her first task was to reconfigure the internal footprint—from a hodge-podge gathering of unrelated rooms to a footprint both logical and livable. We wished to reestablish our home as classic with a contemporary twist and most important, a relaxed vibe. We are old school in many respects and were insistent with Mindy that we not disturb or overplay the home's presence in the established neighborhood but complement it with a new and updated sense of charm."

The owners agreed with Laven that the exterior of the cottage should be refaced around the existing wood-peaked roof as a homage and connection to the home's past, including a series of wood-paneled chevrons beginning with the garage and continuing with the front fence and gate. A Dutch door was added to complete the classic entrance.

OPPOSITE: The chevron woodwork is Mindy's homage to the former cottage as it was transformed into a contemporary cottage.

Flush with natural light, the interior dances with classic and whimsical touches, adding color to the broad white palette of its walls. The main room's fireplace has been constructed with board-formed concrete to exude strength and minimalism while the tile used throughout the kitchen has been hand formed in imperfect shapes to add a hint of unpredictability and honesty to the interior. Of particular interest is a collection of tribal and cross-cultural tribal warriors assembled by the Costa Rican-raised owner, all of which add a sense of gravitas to the otherwise light and warm-hearted cottage.

"We have three very active kids and they have many good friends—all of whom are welcomed at our home—just as our friends were welcomed at our homes as my wife and I were growing up. As for the grown-ups," they add, "we were looking to create a warm and relaxing cottage with a natural feel and Mindy has made it happen with the use of wood floors, a bold concrete fireplace, hand-formed tiles and natural fabric furniture. At the end of the day we sought to create a beautiful home—not one that was showy or overdone. Most of all it needed to reflect a lived-in feeling—no shoes—no shirts—no problem!"

A few weeks after move-in, the owners hosted a celebration of sorts with neighbors and friends and invited Laven. Said the owner, "The party was to celebrate the newly designed cottage but also to celebrate the accomplishment of a fine designer who had listened to us and had quietly worked with us to achieve our goals and objectives." Circling around the large kitchen island that was added for family events such as this, both owners raised their margaritas, a version for which the husband was famous in the neighborhood, and in unison exclaimed, "To Mindy—who has honored this structure—and captured its soul—we honor you—and we thank you!"

ABOVE: The colors, fabrics, textures and patterns are reminiscent of the lively colors of legendary Costa Rican artists Jorge Gallardo and Rafael Angel Fernandez Piedra.

OPPOSITE: Custom wood cabinetry complements the chevron-patterned bathroom floor.

BELOW: Black, white and custom wood cabinetry lends perfect pitch to the bathroom.

RIGHT ABOVE: The acorn represents strength, stability and nobility.

RIGHT BELOW: The polygon black tile completes the black and white bathroom.

Rock-a-bye, baby!

ARTFUL COTTAGE

The purpose of art is washing the dust of daily life off our souls.

—PABLO PICASSO

The search for the perfect cottage took the current owners over two years of combing real estate sections of the local and major dailies, roaming real estate websites and visiting dozens of on-the-market homes. Karen along with her husband, Richard, explains, "Wedged between the pressure of dual careers while seeing our triplets off to college, we persevered with the help of a very patient realtor until one day we received a call to visit a cottage with great potential. My husband, with family roots in old New Orleans and I, with family roots in old California, had strong opinions about the ideal home. His preference was for early-twentieth-century Mission Revival and mine was for midcentury simplicity. What we found the day of that memorable call was a half-century-old cottage, tucked in a unique coastal enclave filled with artists, and a structure that captured our collective vision of raised foundation, plaster walls, open-beamed ceilings, a yard with fruit trees and simple spaces."

From the moment Karen and Richard sealed their purchase, they buffeted each other with ideas, sketches and thoughts on how best to provide their cottage with new life while keeping true to its structure and history. Karen notes, "Aesthetically it was important to maintain a sense of charm and warmth in this gathering place for family and friends. To do that we chose all-natural materials in the form of grass cloth, marble, stone, brick, walnut, glass and cotton and linen textiles." Additionally, their desire for freshness and lightness called for a white palette balanced with contrasting colors and shades. The most obvious contrast was the dark hardwood flooring throughout accented with tastefully selected area rugs to add additional color and contrast.

Karen adds, "We updated some of the charming brick fireplaces by over-grouting them and then painting them white to maintain interior lightness while framing the outer hearth of the living room fireplace with a blue-gray marble. "But it was also important to both of us that we tie our contemporary cottage with selected pieces of furniture from our respective families, some of which were over 100 years old." The placement of the antique furniture was carefully planned and today serves as an anchor to the structure's contemporary uplift.

OPPOSITE: Astier de Villette vases from France complement the grey oak custom Flanders cabinet.

LEFT: Pink peonies are one of many fresh flower arrangements that Karen keeps throughout the cottage.

BELOW: Astier vases sit below an oil painting by William Lees Judson, one of many pieces in Karen and Richard's thoughtfully curated collection of early-twentieth-century plein air paintings installed throughout the cottage.

ABOVE LEFT: One of a pair of grey mist Tuktu chairs, with custom pillow made of bay blue linen from the Rose Tarlow collection, sits near a custom Isabella settee upholstered in Mark Alexander oyster linen.

ABOVE RIGHT: One of Karen's hats pairs nicely with a handsome woven bag and shell necklace.

OPPOSITE: A grey mist Tuktu chairs brightens the living area.

ABOVE: Custom cabinetry in the living room features some of Richard's collection of antiquarian books paired with Karen's collection of antique vases.

OPPOSITE: A custom Cole armchair is upholstered in a Vicenza fabric from the Rose Tarlow collection.

Not to underplay their pride in the rebirth of their cottage from a materials, shades and modern convenience point of view, it is apparent that the crowning touch is the transformation of their cottage into what Karen calls their "artful cottage." "Richard and I had collected early-twentieth-century California plein air art for some time prior to the purchase of our cottage. For us paintings by the likes of Frank Cuprien, William Lees Judson, Edgar Payne, Hanson Puthuff and Dana Bartlett reflect the past beauty, innocence and openness of the coastal region we call home. Though the overall region, with its tens of millions of people, has grown in a way those artists could not have imagined, our immediate artistic community remains intact, protected from twenty-first-century urban pressures by dedicated preserves, greenbelts and the sea. Without any doubt the work of those early-twentieth-century artists remains a source of solace and reflection for Richard and me and is always a point of enjoyment for our guests."

When asked by their friends and visitors alike how they feel as they enter their classic cottage each day after long hours at work, Karen and Richard respond very simply, "The moment we return home we feel warm, reenergized and thankful."

ABOVE: Shaker-inspired white cabinetry is juxtaposed against the richly toned hardwood flooring.

OPPOSITE: An Indonesian hardwood table with contemporary slipper chairs sits
below a custom pendant lamp by Thomas O'Brien in the breakfast nook.

OPPOSITE: Richly toned hardwood floors lead to the formal dining room with woodburning fireplace and a salon-style installation of the couple's early-twentieth-century art collection.

ABOVE: LEFT: An eighteenth-century English walnut breakfront is from the owners' collection.

ABOVE RIGHT: The formal dining room offers a view of the entry and living room.

ABOVE: The iron and marble cocktail table is from Juxtaposition Home.

OPPOSITE: The formal dining room looks out onto a spacious outdoor deck with furniture offered by Restoration Hardware.

BALBOA COTTAGE

My dream is to be on my boat. Or on an island. Or in my house in the country. That's my dream.

—CAMERON MACKINTOSH

For owners Sue and Greg their cottage represents a blend of their love for the country and their bond to the sea. Not long after they were married Greg's career took the California natives to the East Coast where for nearly a decade they immersed themselves in a life in Connecticut—specifically the iconic country village of New Canaan. Sue notes, "While Greg trained each morning into nearby Manhattan, I planned my day around a balance of social events and civic groups. The civic groups focused upon the heritage of the village and nearby hamlets that are both rich in history and tradition and, I might say, quite unlike the traditions with which we grew up in Southern California. Combined with raising a family, those daytime activities were highlighted by our appetite for the cultural gems of nearby New York, its museums, architecture, parks, theatres and shops. It was an unending treasure trove of culture and opportunity that we knew, upon our return to the West Coast, would forever be a part of our choices as they relate to both home and lifestyle."

When one of Greg's competitors came calling with an offer to head an operation in California, the couple lifted their East Coast stakes, but not without acknowledging the permanent impact that life in Connecticut had made upon their lives. Sue explains, "For a time upon our return we lived in a home large enough for a family of five. But as the nest emptied we were determined to combine the best of our experiences back East with a life close to the sea and found our forever cottage tucked amongst others on an island full of history and tradition."

The seaside cottage, originally built in 1932 for a Hollywood film producer as a vacation getaway, has been tastefully redesigned, complete with a nautical entry gate that leads to a welcoming walled garden with bricked patio. Sue notes, "My idea was to convert the small outdoor footprint into an additional living space that was both warm and inviting and accessible from each of the downstairs living areas, providing an indoor-outdoor flow to the cottage capable of being enjoyed throughout the year." She adds, "Our garden is spotted with a wonderful balance of roses and trees for family and dog Gretl to enjoy."

The two-story cottage, though approaching the century mark, today sits as a thoroughly contemporary cottage with its youthful approach to flow, functionality and feel. Says Sue, "My daughter, an established design consultant, worked with me to ensure that each room be inviting—encouraging guests to sit or read. The living room with its use of a comfortable and modern sectional is positioned to take advantage of the woodburning fireplace on foggy evenings, while providing for the flow of guests through our French doors to the outside patio and garden."

Sue proudly notes, "Though I have chosen to minimize clutter within our cottage, choosing discretely the size and scale of each furnishing, Greg and I believe that the soul of a cottage is reflected in its choice of art and family heirlooms. To that end we have thoughtfully chosen to highlight paintings and sculpture we have acquired over time by an eclectic mix of artists including Emil Kosa Jr., Richard Mac-Donald, Chris Gwaltney and Guy Buffet."

RIGHT: The antique and rare cane chairs circling the dining room table have been covered with a traditional ticking—Sue's perfect touch!

BELOW: A medley of dining room views feature "Leaf" wall covering from Katie Ridder.

OPPOSITE: The traditional formal dining room and British-inspired chandelier reflect the couple's love for the East Coast.

The journey from West to East and back again has for Sue and Greg been one that is filled with rich memories and life events, all of which have been called upon by the couple to make their contemporary and forever cottage, though located on an island off the coast of California, imbued with the vitality, richness and tradition of the Connecticut countryside.

ABOVE: The anchor mirror is a century-old piece from the nautical collection of Sue's father.

BELOW: An antique bedroom dresser is constructed of bird's-eye maple.

OPPOSITE: A Jenny Lind spool bed next to a vintage milking stool is in one of the guest bedrooms.

OPPOSITE: One of many antique paintings from Sue's father's collection looks out at a sea foam wicker chair.

ABOVE: An antique bamboo-patterned bed is the center of attention in this colorful guest bedroom.

EAST MEETS WEST COTTAGE

Happiness is not a matter of intensity but of balance, order, rhythm and harmony.

—THOMAS MERTON

With the first step up the vintage brick pathway leading to this inviting West Coast cottage, a home that was raised at the beginning of the last century and redefined nearly ten decades later, one is immediately struck with its East Coast feel, including the sunburst vent providing just the right accent to its gabled roofline. "We had been searching for the perfect cottage in the century-old artist community we now call home when with little fanfare this cottage became available," notes owner Kathy along with husband, Michael. Michael continued, "The previous owner had taken the former aged and tired structure down to its studs and on the original footprint replaced it with a quietly elegant cottage reminiscent of the New England coast, complete with finely crafted cabinetry, raised ceilings and custom architectural features including custom crown molding."

It was important to the couple, Kathy as a designer at heart and Michael as an internationally acclaimed photographer, both of whom were at an achieved stage of their respective careers, that they find a home that reflected their life journey, passion and sensibility. Says Kathy, "Michael and I have Arizona roots. I grew up in a fourth-generation family with a mother and father who took great pride in the exceptionalism and uniqueness of America. Though raising me with a great respect for the American West, its blend of Native American traditions with Spanish and Mexican influences and the achievements of its European settlers, they thought it important that I experience the American East. As a result, every summer of my formative years was spent in Maine

ABOVE: The bold French oak flooring provides a perfect setting for a custom hardwood dining table surrounded by contemporary slipper chairs, a tasteful gold-framed wall mirror, and a traditional chandelier.

OPPOSITE: A contemporary oil painting of the sea sits atop a large English cabinet, which provides Kathy with additional space for storing china and crystal.

where I fell in love with its history. Little did I know that many years later I would join with Michael and our children in sharing the same worldview, passion for art and design sensibility, all of which led us to the cottage that we now call home." Michael continues, "We've lived in several homes throughout our marriage, all of which were special in their own way but none of which brought all of the features and feel we envisioned into a single space. This cottage has achieved the combination of tradition, integrity and charm that we have always sought."

The unhurried comfort of an earlier time is the result of contemporary architectural changes and craftsmanship, the most notable of which is the openness and logical flow of its floor plan. Michael notes, "In 1920s homes, most rooms were for the most part compact, stand alone and low ceilinged. The owner from whom we purchased the cottage removed most of the walls and raised the ceiling. In doing so he allowed sunlight, so abundant in our region, to flood the cottage and fresh sea breezes to fill each room." Adds Kathy, "The previous owner believed in a neutral base

as we do and employed an inviting shade of white throughout the cottage. The vibrancy has been balanced by the introduction of reclaimed hardwood floors throughout, the use of a comfortably sheen black shade on large hanging sconces in the kitchen, the introduction of blue and green textiles the color of the sea and indigenous objects from every trip we've made to countries around the world." Michael gleefully interjects, "And despite all of the structural changes the casement windows are original to the cottage complete with wavy glass and a refurbished rope and pulley system!" Finally, as Kathy notes, "The introduction of color upon the white palette is achieved at its best by the artisan landscaping and choice of blooms just outside each window. We are surrounded by nature's reds, pinks, blues, violets, yellows and greens. Outside colors are drawn into each room in the most vibrant way!"

What Kathy and Michael call their "collected home" is a cottage that was built in one century and reborn in another but one that has maintained a single purpose—to provide their children, guests and themselves with a sense of warmth and harmony achieved by a confluence of the best of East with the best of the West.

A vibrant and inviting master bedroom with custom sitting nook lends a bright view of the cottage's garden.

OPPOSITE: The custom grey Roman window covering lends shade to a Gustavian writing desk and custom upholstered matching chair.

ABOVE: Contemporary lighting has been installed throughout the eighty-year-old cottage.

BELOW: Vintage paintings handed down to Kathy and Michael by their respective families.

OPPOSITE: The custom French doors in the redesigned guest bedroom provide guests with access to an outdoor sitting deck and garden view. The bed is dressed with a custom duvet and curated custom pillows from the Tuvalu Home collection.

ABOVE LEFT: A century-old table provides old and new contrasts within the guest bedroom.

ABOVE RIGHT: Kathy wished to provide her contemporary cottage with vintage touches and nothing is more vintage and comfortable than this freestanding claw-foot tub reminiscent of a Cotswolds cottage.

OPPOSITE: The courtyard offers hardwood Adirondack chairs designed with a contemporary flair.

LEFT: Kathy and Michael worked with their landscape architect to provide a sitting area in the yard that encourages quiet contemplation.

BELOW: A magnificent sawbuck table surrounded by a dozen vintage chairs sourced from a French antique dealer provides a large outdoor dining space for family and guests.

BOUNTIFUL COTTAGE

Blessed are those who see beautiful things in humble places where other people see nothing.

—CAMILLE PISSARRO

For Bountiful homeowner Ashley Clark, the roots of beautiful things and their impact on her career as an interior designer first took shape at the base of the majestic Wasatch Range in Utah. "As early as I can remember the scents, sounds and majesty of the Wasatch Mountains had a special influence on me, especially in the spring and autumn. Spring is a time for new life in the Rockies. Though a city girl, I made regular trips to my grandparents' dairy farm where I learned to bond with the beauty and color of the land. I learned the value of hard work and accomplishment—traits that have continued to define my drive to succeed with both family and career. In autumn, the green of high-country aspen groves turned to gold, orange and red—complementing the vivid gold of cottonwoods that lined the streams. The abundance of natural shades and color gave me an early lesson in the use and presence of color and has been an integral part of my design sensibility."

Following a family tradition, Clark studied at Utah State, earning a degree in marketing but always maintaining a strong interest in design. With post-graduate financial responsibilities knocking at the door, she pivoted to real estate and finance. It was the switch to real estate that returned her to design with a focus on interiors. "I had a client who, after seeing some of my design work at a visit to my home, requested that I work with her on a new home she had in mind—on condition that I close the sale on her current home. That was all the incentive I needed. We closed the deal and within a month it was off to the races with my first design project. The rest is history!"

Clark's work on her own home included more than design—it involved a structural re-do that was, at the time, new territory for her. "I loved the quarter-century-old property but I soon realized that if it was going to be the permanent home for my husband and our family of four it was going to need some significant structural changes. We love the flow and feel of a single-story home and wanted to avoid an upstairs-downstairs arrangement." The original cottage's 1,800-square-foot footprint was reconfigured to 2,500 square feet, including Clark's repurposing of what was once an outside courtyard into indoor living space. "From the street it appears to be a modest charmer with a small footprint but upon entering our guests are astounded at its breadth and depth. It immediately opens to a space that showers each visitor with an abundance of natural light, illuminating the beauty and warmth of the interior while at the same time drawing upon the natural beauty of well-planned and tended landscaping." Ensuring natural light was no small task, and Clark's choice of an abundance of windows and French doors has guaranteed a seamless blend of inside and outside living.

Her high-country roots are apparent the moment a visitor walks into the entryway where the cottage's theme of light hardwood contrasts against white brick, illuminated with powerful industrial ceiling lights that are painted black for additional contrast. Each guest then passes through a large floor-to-ceiling slider into a modern living and dining area, which, though minimalist in its design, is made warm and inviting by the furniture and interior elements selected by Clark. "The entry and slider when taken together are a homage to my grandparents' barn and dairy farm and the special days I spent with them growing up."

For her home Clark chose colors to contrast light and dark—choosing a Benjamin Moore color called "Jet" which she describes as a "smoky dark gray." It is used on the trim, the kitchen island, bathroom cabinets and two bedrooms, including a powerful master bedroom wall. While choosing to employ a clean, neutral and uncluttered look throughout her home, she has added some special touches, not the least of which is a vintage 1940s basketball scoreboard that she had rewired and installed in her son's bedroom.

OPPOSITE: Twenty-first-century chairs contrast against a kitchen island painted with Benjamin Moore "Jet" in a clean-lined kitchen space.

ABOVE: Ashley has an extensive collection of antique wood utensils and bowls.

BELOW: A casual lifestyle is captured in the informal dining area with a modern motif light fixture.

ABOVE: The Benjamin Moore "Jet" black accentuates the master bedroom furnishings.

OPPOSITE: A Persian runner in the master bath with Jack-and-
Jill vanities reflects Ashley's love for the unexpected.

Was the multiyear project worth the effort? "Yes—and more! But having said that, I quickly learned that being a homeowner and designer is much harder than it sounds! Making design decisions for yourself—your own home—is hard! So, while in my business I am inspired by the Napa Valley designer Erin Martin, Pittsburgh's Leanne Ford, and the Los Angeles-based designer Eric Olsen, I can't adequately describe the admiration I have for Diane Keaton who, as a homeowner, has designed and redesigned her homes in a creative fashion and in doing so has, through her work and books, empowered homeowners who wish to introduce a degree of individuality and uniqueness into their homes and living spaces."

Ashley's career has taken some surprising turns, including the successful design of her own home. It is certain that future projects will reflect her belief that nothing is more rewarding than respectfully taking a space that may have become static after years of family enjoyment and breathing into it new life and purpose.

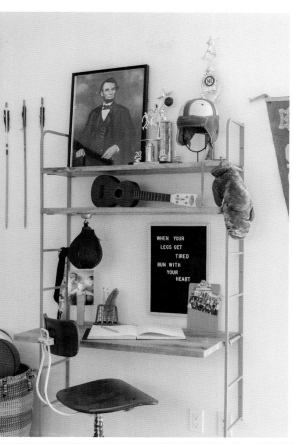

OPPOSITE: Ashley has a passion for all things natural and nothing is more compelling than the natural fiber rug in her son's room, complete with dynamic patterns.

LEFT: There's always room for toys.

BELOW: A children's room with smartly wooded cabinetry surrounded by matching twin beds sports unique headboards composed of oversized lumbar ticking patterned pillows attached to the wall with leather straps.

ABOVE: The vintage sawbuck table and airy natural towel cabinet sit ready to accommodate guests taking advantage of the outside living and pool area.

OPPOSITE: Crosby circles the pool before his daily dip.

HIGHLANDS COTTAGE

Beauty is the harmony of purpose and form.

—ALVAR AALTO

itting atop a bluff with the sea nearby and less than a mile from where one of its owners grew up, this contemporary cottage has been transformed into a harmonious blend of purpose and form. "Having recently graduated with degrees in business from the same university and flush with common interests, energy and goals, Tom and I launched a determined search for an existing home that possessed the right combination of space, light and potential, elements for us to create a bright and clean-lined contemporary cottage," notes owner, Michelle. "When we came upon this sixty-year-old structure we looked beyond 'now' and envisioned 'then'—agreeing on what we needed to do to accommodate the day when not only the two of us, but our children, would call this place our home."

The herringboned brick walkway is surrounded by a carefully crafted landscape filled with drought-resistant foliage and airy trees and leads to a welcoming eave-covered entryway. Michelle notes, "Our intent was to provide a clean, Nantucket-like feel to the property and with the grey acid-washed shingles exterior we have accomplished that goal. In fact, the sea has an impact on the exterior as well as interior. While I was growing up, my Dad was passionate about sailing and it had an impact on the whole family. He saw it as an ideal way to stay healthy and youthful and to connect with nature and sea life in all its forms. In a way our design sensibility is a homage to that unforgettable childhood."

"Our home has a traditional look driven by a nontraditional layout. We inherited a 1,200-square-foot space that we have expanded to 3,000 square feet with the addition of a second floor—larger by nearly a factor of three yet warm, open, light and inviting," says Michelle. "We kept to the spirit of the original floor plan but improved the flow between rooms, including the removal of one wall on the first floor to make way for an open kitchen that looks into a bright and fresh great room. Being a design purist, I built upon a neutral redesign complemented with clean lines, understated hardware, traditional millwork, white marble and modern lighting."

"The floors are French oak. The walls were painted with Benjamin Moore's 'China White.' Contrast is found by way of colored and striped textiles, textured floor coverings, sturdy vintage tables, textured window coverings, vintage paintings and a pair of well-worn leather chairs."

ABOVE: Custom pendant lighting hangs above an informal dining area that looks through to the formal dining room.

BELOW: The contemporary wood stools are designed to offer a bold complement to the Benjamin Moore "China White" interior.

OPPOSITE: Michelle's favorite reading nook is completed with custom fabric indigo pillows from the Juxtaposition Home collection.

OPPOSITE: The French oak hardwood floors extend into the kitchen and provide a vintage contrast to the contemporary kitchen cabinetry.

ABOVE LEFT: Michelle is an admirer of the Astier de Villette collection from France.

ABOVE RIGHT: The cabinetry is contemporary as well as finely crafted to fit into the newly designed kitchen area.

"To add a sense of surprise, one of the bedrooms is done in shiplap and another is painted a bold navy blue. I grew up in a house where the rooms were identified by their respective colors and I wanted to bring a bit of that tradition into our home."

Michelle concludes, "When I share with others the meaning of 'cottage' it is not as a design concept or expression of style but a reflection of family, growth and tradition." With Highlands Cottage it is clear that Michelle and husband, Tom, have achieved in their home a harmony of both purpose and form.

OPPOSITE: Michelle and Tom, with careers in real estate and finance, make full use of this small work area—efficient and yet understated so as not to detract from the main purpose of their cottage, which is living with family and entertaining friends.

ABOVE: Michelle has chosen to decorate her cottage with carefully chosen wall pieces including black-and-white photographs.

RIGHT: With new architectural changes to the cottage came an abundance of shelving upon which to feature collected pieces and family heirlooms.

PRAIRIE HOME

In a way I spend my entire life stealing from everything—from the past, from cities I love, from where I grew up—grabbing things, taking not only from architecture . . . but art, writing, poetry, music.

—RENZO PIANO

Shannon McLaren Wilkins has lived and studied here and around the globe. "It's not lost on me how influential colleagues and friends, many from different nations, cultures and social circumstances, have been and the influence they've had on me as a parent and as a designer. Where they've offered thoughts I've gladly grabbed them! The overwhelming diversity of ideas to which I've been exposed in Los Angeles, along with the influences of Seattle, the frenetic and creative energy of New York and the seething creativity through all of London, has opened my eyes to the infinite possibilities in both personal styling and residential design."

Though subsequently sold by Shannon to a successor family, her cottage was an exciting project as an owner-designer. According to Wilkins, the original interior featured dark woods and river rock with a very traditional feel. "I looked beyond the traditional and was immediately struck with the beauty of the cottage's bones—its basic footprint—its floor plan—a perfect single-floor setting within which to establish, along with the sleeping quarters for my growing family, a light-filled main room, kitchen, dining and living area, all of which open up to a spacious half-acre of grounds—a very substantial setting in an otherwise tight urban environment.

"We are a very active family with all of the demands that come along with it. I wanted to maximize the use of living space, for my husband's office needs as well as visiting neighborhood kids." Keeping that in mind, the interior was transformed into a Scandinavian-inspired twenty-first-century space. "Cautious to avoid the 'white box' dilemma facing many 'new-vibe' homes, I elected to counterbalance its whiteness by employing a powerful shade of black throughout the home's trim and bathroom tile—but the

ABOVE: Shannon's uninhibited and creative use of space, vibrant colors and textures contrasted against a palate of white and black has gained her industry-wide attention and the acclaim of clients.

OPPOSITE: Pink, red and salmon dyes integrated with stark black patterns and borders of this large runner provide exciting contrast to the hallway's clean palate and light hardwood flooring.

most apparent use of black is a 35-foot-long slider that opened our home to the half-acre yard. Sliders are becoming more prevalent in current design plans but to my knowledge no one has installed a 35-foot slider. It's truly dynamic."

In addition to the black-and-white "counterpunch," Wilkins placed eclectic pieces of art throughout the home to add a sense of color and action to the baseline design scheme. "As both owner and designer the project left me with a sense of accomplishment and a desire to parlay the success with my own home to future projects—and I have not been disappointed!"

Whether as an owner-designer or commissioned designer, Shannon continues to exhibit a pitch-perfect ability to turn the design of traditional cottages into that of the new century.

OPPOSITE ABOVE: Shannon's sensibility pivots to stark uses of black and white tones softened with the positioning of vintage planters in her client conference room.

OPPOSITE BELOW: A black wall provides a dynamic gallerylike ambiance to the paintings and other art pieces in the client conference room.

ABOVE: Shannon's employment of soft, inviting blue upholstered contemporary chairs around a centered conference table on an impressive curated woven rug, puts clients in plain view of a tribal-design wall hanging and tribal-design wallpaper, reminding them of her passion for global design.

ABOVE: Contemporary steel stools juxtaposed with traditional wood
stools surround the open kitchen on the main floor.

OPPOSITE: A traditional table with curated chairs for twelve are positioned under
a contemporary sconce chandelier in an open dining and living area.

ABOVE: Custom shelving displays some of the extensive collection of books and art pieces.

OPPOSITE: Shannon's design genius for blending unexpected patterns, colors and designs into an integrated jewel is highlighted in this guest entertainment area with a specially designed steel coffee table.

ABOVE LEFT: A free-flowing natural wood slider opens to a masculine bedroom.

ABOVE RIGHT: Another free-flowing slider opens to a feminine bedroom.

OPPOSITE: A third free-flowing natural wood slider opens to a guest bathroom just off a guest room complete with full-bed convertible under a dynamic custom chandelier, the fingers of which are constructed of hand-turned wood.

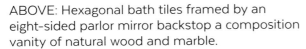

ABOVE: Hexagonal bath tiles framed by an eight-sided parlor mirror backstop a composition vanity of natural wood and marble.

RIGHT: The en suite master bathroom is a symphony of Rorschach-patterned black-and-white tile with a double-headed French shower on one end of the room and a French bateau pedestal tub on the other.

BERKSHIRES COTTAGE

I left the woods for as good a reason as I went there. Perhaps it seemed to me that I had several more lives to live and could not spare any more time for that one.

—HENRY DAVID THOREAU

Having met while attending USC in Los Angeles, Greg, a native Californian and Pennsylvania-raised sociologist, and Clark, a southern Californian with a background in design and finance, were drawn to Massachusetts and life in the Berkshires in the early 2000s. Clark had previously gained valuable experience working under the iconic designer Michael Smith known for his rigorous focus on the minutest of details required in the pursuit of preservation and restoration. While Greg taught at prestigious Williams College, Clark worked to combine the experience and client base that today has made him a leading residential designer and developer. Life for the couple in those early days was idyllic as they found themselves surrounded with an overabundance of history, culture and architectural beauty, both within historic Williamstown and nearby Berkshires hamlets and extending to the countryside of upstate New York and Vermont.

It is the strong influence of the Berkshires that led the couple and their growing family to Berkshires Cottage. Says Clark, "Our passion for older and historic homes led us to this cottage that had been for years terribly neglected and in a sorry state." Greg adds," We immediately envisioned it as a cottage that, with hard work and patience, could be brought back to life with contemporary standards and functionality while leaving undisturbed a uniqueness that was the product of an artist's vision and hard work nearly a century before." And that is exactly what the couple did by moving in and shortly thereafter moving out to make way for what was to be a full year of design, refresh, improvement and in some instances rebuild, including a full replumb and rewiring. "We either refurbished and repaired period pieces and fixtures or did our best to employ original

period pieces and fixtures to ensure the historical integrity of our cottage," Clark notes. "It was a full year of contemporizing what is best described as a hybrid blend of cottage, cabin and barn."

As one faces the property and its inviting wooded lot, the view is nothing short of spectacular with entry on a series of tiered stone steps through an arbor-covered custom gate that leads uphill to the front door. The door is to the right of a massive top-rounded picture window above which sits a New England sunburst vent, both of which are original to the cottage. "The original owner-builder wanted a sweeping view of the front property but overlooked the effect of sunlight on the cottage's temperature. We took care of it with the addition of ventilation windows just below the picture window without diminishing one bit the magnificence of the picture window," Clark says.

The beamed ceiling in the living room exceeds fifteen feet, providing space to the otherwise warm and inviting living room. "The cedar-lined walls and fir floors are original to the cottage," Clark adds. Greg interjects, "An interesting historical note—as we took to refurbishing the walls we had to remove several hundred old nails, from which, we are told, the original artist-owner hung his own paintings salon style and those of his artist colleagues and friends. It was in many ways a home and a gallery and we are told it was the scene of many artist meetings, both professional and social." Clark and Greg have continued the tradition with original pieces tastefully hung throughout the cottage by early-twentieth-century artists such as Anna Hills, Frank Cuprien, Clarence Hinkle and Dedrick Stuber.

Leading from the spacious living room is a dual staircase up to a reading loft. Clark notes, "All of us have favorite spots in the cottage—our sons migrate to the reading loft and I love the originally upholstered mohair couch from the workshop of England's George Smith Ltd., enjoying either the 1930s reflections of Steinbeck or the more recent humor of David Sedaris." He continues, "As for Greg—in addition to his professional interests, his passion is the creation of unique dishes. He is the *chef de la maison* in a portion of the cottage that was redesigned on his vision to accommodate a fully equipped modern and professional kitchen."

"As the son of a sturdy and hardworking family with Polish roots I have also introduced my family to hearty Polish recipes that they especially enjoy during the holidays," Greg proudly declares.

Historic with a contemporary twist, Berkshires Cottage is not only Greg and Clark's contribution to the architectural tradition of the artistic community in which they live but to the legacy that their children will one day inherit and nurture as they follow in their parents' footsteps.

ABOVE: What once was a simple sitting room has been expanded into a dynamic open-air kitchen and eating area that maintains the historic feel of the cottage while providing a space for Clark to prepare his traditional back-East family dishes.

OVERLEAF: The reading room just off the main living room provides ample space for entertaining or enjoyment of a good book near the fireplace.

OPPOSITE: The master bedroom with its vintage English leather headboard and matching footboard is accented with Indigo custom lumbar pillows, a 1920s inspired fixture and one of many notable vintage paintings found throughout the cottage.

ABOVE: The double vanity with a decidedly masculine feel is topped with custom marble.

RIGHT: An antique rug, early American table and vintage oil painting sit near the door leading from the main cottage to the enclosed porch at the back of the cottage.

OPPOSITE: A beautifully crafted outdoor porch unites life within and outside the main cottage.

ORCHID COTTAGE

One new feature or fresh take can change everything.

—NEIL YOUNG

O rchid Cottage, a newly constructed getaway for a young couple and their four children, sits within a century-old and highly regarded seaside neighborhood that is peppered with both new and original early-twentieth-century cottages and homes. The owner notes, "The project was a total collaboration between our architect, our designer and us to ensure that our goal of a light, airy and organic space was achieved while blending harmoniously with the look and scale of the nearby cottages and homes of our neighbors. We wished for the space to be sophisticated and yet approachable. We achieved that feel by employing unique materials and lighting throughout the living areas, kitchen/dining and bedrooms, including reclaimed beams, wide-oak hardwood flooring and millwork that is the result of second-to-none artisanship."

The cottage is the work of architect Cynthia Childs and is heavily influenced by the owners' longtime interest in a New England sensibility. It is open and warm with an abundance of natural light. "We wanted a vacation home in a temperate zone and this cottage has all the benefits of a Mediterranean climate. We've chosen French doors, exposed closets and cabinetry throughout our cottage to allow us to break down the distinction between outdoor and indoor living year-round. Architecturally, it sports a flow and functionality that provides maximum enjoyment for our children and us."

The interior of the cottage was designed by Kelly Nutt and is appointed throughout with a collection of classic furniture and textiles. "Kelly knows us well—our old-school sensibility—and we were happy to employ her suggestions highlighting classic stripes and seersucker, which added a layer of tradition to the new structure. We selected art by

PREVIOUS OVERLEAF: From its hand-hewn ceiling beams to oak flooring, the inviting living area is a contrast of eclectic textiles tucked amongst its fresh and vibrant upholstered furniture.

ABOVE: The aged kitchen space has been beautifully modernized with Shaker-like lines and cabinetry.

BELOW: A twenty-first-century custom chandelier above a breakfast nook was added with the cottage's redesign.

OPPOSITE: The addition of hand-hewn beams and an oven hood covered with aged wood is a pitch-perfect touch contrasting vintage with contemporary.

abstract mixed media artist Lorraine Pennington who provided just the right pitch to balance our old-school vibe with a twenty-first-century contemporary feel." Nutt, a product of the American South, but with college and a career on the West Coast, worked for over a decade with the Ralph Lauren organization specializing in home design, and successfully brought to the owners' table the mantra expressed by Mr. Lauren to employees and customers alike: "I design for the home the way I design for a man or a woman, with the same attention to detail and the same eye for what is beautiful and unique."

The owners note, "We are happy to share visits to our new cottage with family and friends, and trust that those visits leave them with the same sense of warmth and joy that we have come to experience each day as its proud owners."

ABOVE: Aged hand-hewn beams, a contemporary teardrop chandelier and upholstered white dining chairs under a dark antique dining table provide modern drama.

OPPOSITE ABOVE: Clean-lined and comfortable club chairs contrast with a bold forgelike circular custom chandelier.

OPPOSITE BELOW: The French oak floors extend to the stairs leading to the second floor.

ABOVE: A bright and well-textured guest room is always inviting.

RIGHT: The second floor reflects the owners' tastes and accommodates a master bedroom and bathroom with a vibrant layering of colors, textures and wall art.

A room with flexibility, complete with a woodburning fireplace, can be used as a bedroom or sitting room.

RIGHT: Clean Shaker-like lines enhance one of several bathrooms.

BELOW: A children's room—reminiscent of an Adirondack lodge from the 1930s—is completed with vintage camp pennants and blankets.

OPPOSITE: An additional child's room features colors, textures and fixtures suggestive of a royal room in the 1953 Oscar-winning movie *Roman Holiday*.

HARMONY HILL COTTAGE

Harmony is best achieved through a balance of dreams, thoughts and imagination; dreaming only of what is best from the past, thinking through and taking ownership of the day's opportunities and setting aside quiet moments to imagine a purposeful future.

—ANONYMOUS

"There are times when a searcher ends up being the one who is found!" exclaims the owner of this charming 1930s cottage. She continues, "My adult daughter and son had just begun their own life journeys when I was suddenly faced with continuing mine on my own, which I elected to do with a sense of strength and purpose. One day while on a new home search with a friend, I came upon what I instantly knew was the place that would become my new home—a white-shingled contemporary cottage sitting on a rising hill, surrounded by an abundant preservelike setting of flora and songbirds. Just when I thought I had been the person searching for a new home I realized that instead the cottage on the hill had found me!"

Tucked in a grove of old-growth trees and accessible by way of a half-century-old brick path, the eighty-year-old cottage has, with the help of designer Andra Miller, been provided with new life without losing the unique characteristics and charm of an earlier century. The high-beamed living room ceiling retains a sense of cottage warmth while introducing a sense of openness to take advantage of the early morning sunlight. "Some of the features found in cottages of the past century are in many ways without equal to today's homes," she notes. "For instance, the original owner built a whimsical bed into a closeted alcove! When guests come, they fight over the room—they tell me that it reminds them of their childhood days at sleepaway camp."

She continues, "Growing up I was the youngest and the only girl amongst several boys. My world revolved around my brothers and their friends, including boy sports. I was a 'tom-girl' in the truest sense, adventuresome and rambunctious. Yet I was a girl with my own sense of fashion and design, a sense that was predictably softer than the crash of a baseball that every once in a while ripped through a neighbor's window—I have always felt that I was born to create."

The open kitchen and dining area is a panoply of color and style.

With constant companion Gunner, a ten-year-old yellow lab retriever, at her side, she has built upon that youthful sensibility with the introduction of contemporary furniture, art and colorful textiles in blues, teals and citrons. She notes, "When my son and daughter, especially my daughter with her pup, Atlas, a Nova Scotia duck tolling retriever, arrive for weekend dinner, Harmony Hill becomes a cottage filled with happiness and love—as it was always meant to be!"

The great American dancer Agnes de Mille once said, "No trumpets sound when the important decisions of our life are made. Destiny is made known silently." So it has been with this owner who, despite her challenges, was one day suddenly "found" by Harmony Hill, a contemporary cottage that has provided her with a renewed sense of achievement, love and happiness.

OPPOSITE: The powerful chandelier above the table, and the chair coverings in the informal dining area represent the owner's bold use of color throughout the white interior.

ABOVE LEFT: The yellow chairs tucked under the kitchen island is another indication of the owner's love of color.

ABOVE RIGHT: Natural sunlight streams through every window and French door.

OPPOSITE: Neptune and the sea inspired this beautifully decorated master bedroom.

ABOVE: The Jack-and-Jill vanity features beautifully crafted cabinetry.

BELOW: The vintage-inspired bathtub is every woman's retreat.

ABOVE: The bold star and subway tile combination makes showering fun.

OPPOSITE: The blue burst-patterned tiles contrast wonderfully with the stand-alone vanity.

WOODS COVE COTTAGE

We are torn between nostalgia for the familiar and an urge for the foreign and strange. As often as not, we are homesick most for the places we have never known.

—CARSON MCCULLERS

For James and Arabella Cant, he a professional photographer in Melbourne and she a music industry art director/consultant in London, any thought just a few short years ago of breathing new life into a 1933 cottage on the West Coast of the U.S. would have been pure fiction. But fate and chance often take us where we least expect it, and for the couple it was a visit to the U.S. and an enchanting neighborhood called Woods Cove where they met and fell in love with a cottage yearning to be reborn. "Though I chose a career in professional photography, I come from a family of builders, property developers and engineers—four generations worth—blessed with a critical eye as it relates to redeveloping and redefining older structures," James notes. "Combined with Arabella's world-class artistic and promotional talents, including a stint with *World of Interiors* magazine in London, we were determined to provide the cottage with the attentive detail necessary not only to bring it back to life but to fashion it as an extraordinary contemporary space while staying true to its past."

The 1,750-square-foot cottage, with its footprint intact, was, during the year-long project, reduced to its old-growth studs. The cottage has an H-shaped design. The set of rooms associated with living and the set dedicated to dining and entertaining are at opposite ends of a long hallway, with Jack-and-Jill bedrooms and a shared bathroom just off the connecting hallway. The front Dutch door entry is on the southeast side of the hallway. Off the entry the couple have turned what was originally a formal room into

a master suite, bathroom and reading room with additional bathroom. "Redesigning what was once a formal room into an open master bedroom with nearby reading room and bathroom for each was, for us, a more contemporary and functional use of the space," James notes. "A special feature made possible by the room's reuse is the en suite woodburning fireplace—a feature not normally associated with old cottages." Arabella adds, "We were particularly pleased with our idea of extending the flow of the master bedroom into a private reading room facing the secluded courtyard in the rear of the cottage. It has a special feeling—open and yet private."

ABOVE: Small black diamond-patterned tile makes a statement in a guest bathroom.

OPPOSITE: A beautifully crafted nineteenth-century chest sits outside the master bathroom.

ABOVE: The open-air dining area plays host to a large dining table complete with contemporary wood chairs that play off the beautiful chevron-shaped French oak hardwood floors.

RIGHT: The open-air kitchen and sitting area are complemented by a contemporary island and sleek steel chairs for additional seating.

The northwest to southeast hallway, connecting the two major living spaces, is flooded with natural sunlight pouring through multiple sets of wood-paned windows, below which sit custom-crafted shelving that is home to their well-curated collection of art, photography and design books and journals.

At the northwest end of the hallway the couple have redesigned what was originally a living area into an open and airy dining and entertainment area. Arabella notes, "We keep the French doors wide open while at home to take advantage of the mild on-shore breezes." The doors lead to a small but comfortable outdoor sitting area with firepit, surrounded by landscaping to ensure privacy. The open galley kitchen along with the carefully designed island, indoor dining area and outdoor sitting area, combine to make the entire space an en plein air dining experience. After dinner, guests make their way to the newly designed formal room, with bathroom, just off the dining area and facing the private courtyard.

The couple is proud to have employed what James calls "extreme discipline and clever engineering" in their redesign project. It was the artist Max Ernst who once said, "Creativity is that marvelous capacity to grasp mutually distinct realities and draw a spark from their juxtaposition." Such is the creativity that James and Arabella have employed with the rebirth of Woods Cove Cottage.

The family room and connecting hallway French doors open onto a private and high-fenced courtyard perfect for personal reflection, dining or entertaining.

OPPOSITE: The family enjoys this comfortable family room with woodburning fireplace.

ABOVE: John sits at the foot of Arabella's club chair upholstered with her native Union Jack.

RESOURCES

STORES

Blue Springs Home
369 E. 17th Street
Costa Mesa, CA 92627
(949) 642-3632
Website: www.bluespringshome.com
Instagram: blue springs home

Brass Tack
311 Ocean Avenue
Laguna Beach, CA 92651
(949) 715-0310
Email: Melissa@brasstackstudio.com
Instagram: brass_tack

Camps and Cottages
1233 N. Coast Hwy.
Laguna Beach, CA 92651
(949) 494-2100
Email: campsncottages@aol.com
Website: camps-cottages.com
Instagram: camps and cottages

Huit Laguna
1492 S. Coast Hwy. #8
Laguna Beach, CA 92651
(949) 715-5617
Email: huitlaguna@gmail.com
Website: huitlaguna.com
Instagram: huitlaguna

Juxtaposition Home
7976 E. Coast Hwy.
Newport Beach, CA 92657
(949) 715-1181
Email: info@juxtapostionhome.com
Website: juxtaposition.com
Instagram: juxtapositionhome

Melange
1235 N. Coast Hwy.
Laguna Beach, CA 92651
(949) 497-4915

Patine
1001 41st Avenue
Santa Cruz, CA 95062
(831) 464-0950
Email: danii@patinedecor.com
Website: euro-linens.com
Instagram: patine

Solo
309 S. Cedros
Solana Beach, CA 92075
(858) 794-9016
Website: www.solocedros.com
Instagram: solocedros

Tancredi & Morgen
7174 Carmel Valley Road
Carmel, CA 93923
(831) 625-4477
Email: megan@tancredimorgen.com
Website: tancrediandmorgen.com
Instagram: tancredimorgen

Tuvalu Home
295 Forest Ave.
Laguna Beach, CA 92651
(949) 497-3202

222 N. El Camino Real
San Clemente, CA 92672
(949) 542-8242

Upstairs at Pierre La Fond
516 San Ysidro Rd.
Montecito, CA 93108
(805) 565-1503
Email: upstairs@wendyfoster.com
Website: shopupstairs.com
Instagram: upstairspierrelafond

Vertigo Home
1550 S. Coast Hwy.
Laguna Beach, CA 92651
(949) 494-7547
Email: info@vertigohome.us.com
Website: vertigohome.us
Instagram: vertigohomelaguna

The Warmth Company
140 Post Office Drive
Aptos, CA 95003
(831) 688-3200

1003 41st Avenue
Santa Cruz, CA 95062
(831) 515-2704
Website: warmthcompany.com
Instagram: warmthcompany

DESIGNERS

Ashley Clark, Skout Design
Website: shopskout.com
Instagram: shopskout

Andra Miller
Email: Andra.r.Miller@gmail.com

Clark Collins
Email: clark@collinsone.net
Instagram: collinsdevelopment

Kelly Nutt Design
Website: Kellynuttdesign.com
Instagram: kellynuttdesign

Laurie Alter
Website: Tuvaluhome.com
Instagram: tuvaludesign

Mindy Laven Home
Website: mindylaven.com
Instagram: mindylavenhome

Molly Wood Garden Design
1660 Orange Ave.
Costa Mesa, CA 92627
(949) 548-1611
Website: mollywoodgardendesign.com

Raili Clasen
Website: railiCAdesign.com
Instagram: raili_ca_design

Shannon Willkins, Prairie Home Design
Website: prairiehomestyling.com
Instagram: prairie_home_styling

CUSTOM TEXTILES

Textile Repair Studio
Email: info@quiltrepair.com
(510) 548-2267

Tricot Naturelle
Email: naturalknitting@icloud.com
Instagram: Tricot_naturelle

FLORAL STYLING

Kate Jeremias
Email: ksjflora@gmail.com
Instagram: flora_workshop

PHOTOGRAPHER

Ryan Garvin
Website: ryangarvin.com
Instagram: ryangarvin

ARCHITECTS

Bob White
Www.Foreststudio.com

Cynthia Childs Architect
Www.ccarchitect.com

Eric Olsen
Www.ericolsendesign.com

Tim Nicol
Www.nicolarchitecture.com

THE AUTHOR

Molly Hyde English has been a longtime passionate purveyor and proponent of curated and vintage textiles, art and interior items and their eclectic mix within modern and contemporary settings. A graduate of California State University at Long Beach, Molly began her career with the airlines as a sales executive with three major carriers in several principal U.S. cities and thereafter as a marketing director with a large California state agency, major land transport company and regional entertainment company. It was while living in the San Francisco Bay Area that she moved from corporate sales and marketing into retail, establishing Camps and Cottages. She moved her store to the greater Los Angeles area in the early 2000s, where it has continued to draw retail customers and designer clients from throughout the region as well as loyal followers throughout the U.S. who follow her on Instagram and her website www.camps-cottages.com. She shared her passion and work mixing vintage with contemporary in her first book, *Camps and Cottages* (Gibbs Smith), in 2000 and later with *Vintage Cottages* (Gibbs Smith) in 2007. With *Contemporary Cottages*, Molly has set forth a photographic chronicle with owner and designer thoughts underlying the transformation of "cottage" from a traditional "vintage" space to one marked by lightness, energy and a fast-paced twenty-first-century sensibility. The trilogy provides readers with a thoughtful appreciation of the continuing role that cottages play on the American scene.

THE PHOTOGRAPHER

Ryan Garvin is an interior design photographer based in Southern California. He began his photography career nearly a decade ago, and honed his aesthetic in the process of putting in his "10,000 hours." He pays special attention to horizontal and vertical lines with his work, and he seeks out the interesting and thoughtful details at each shoot. Relying almost entirely on natural light, he prides himself on the photographic style he has come to be known for. His work can be seen in notable print and web publications, ranging from *Elle Decor* to *Traditional Home,* and most often—your Integra feed. Prior to photography, he was working in ministry and had initially thought a career in children's ministry would be his path.